MW01102256

Gift of Steve Sanborn
in memory of his brother, Robert

NOW HIRING: TRAVEL

by Deborah Crisfield

Crestwood House
New York

Maxwell Macmillan Canada
Toronto

Maxwell Macmillan International
New York   Oxford   Singapore   Sydney

Copyright © 1994 by Crestwood House, Macmillan Publishing Company

Crestwood House
Macmillan Publishing Company
866 Third Avenue
New York, NY 10022

Maxwell Macmillan Canada, Inc.
1200 Eglinton Avenue East
Suite 200
Don Mills, Ontario M3C 3N 1

Macmillan Publishing Company is part of the Maxwell Communication
Group of Companies.

Produced by Twelfth House Productions
Designed by R Studio T
cover: travel agent, Brian Vaughan; curbside check-in, American Airlines: cruise ship, Carnival Cruise Lines
Carnival Cruise Lines: 5, 36–37, 39
Brian Vaughan: 7
Japan National Tourist Organization: 13
United Airlines: 16, 17, 33
Courtesy of the Marriott Marquis: 21, 23
Courtesy of Holland America Line Tours: 26
Danny Lehman, courtesy of Holland America Line Tours: 28
French Government Tourist Office: 42–43

First Edition

Printed in the United States of America

10   9   8   7   6   5   4   3   2   1

Library of Congress Cataloging-in-Publication Data

Crisfield, Deborah.
    Travel / by Deborah Crisfield.—1st ed.
        p.   cm.—(Now hiring)
    Includes index.
    Summary: A behind-the-scenes look at different types of careers
available in the travel industry.
    ISBN 0-89686-790-0
    1. Tourist trade—Vocational guidance—Juvenile literature.
2. Travel agents—Vocational guidance—Juvenile literature.   3. Tour
guides (persons)—Vocational guidance—Juvenile literature.
[1. Tourist trade.   2. Travel agents.   3. Tour guides (persons).
4. Vocational guidance.]   I. Title.   II. Series: Now hiring.
G155.5.C75   1994
338.4′791023—dc20   93-15211

CONTENTS

THIS BUSINESS OF TRAVEL

The world is a very big place, and there are millions of great places to visit. You could spend a lifetime traveling and still not see all the sights on earth. And while doing all this traveling, you could also spend a lot of money.

Fortunately, there is another way to see the world. And you can actually earn money instead of spending it. It's a job in the travel industry. Airlines, cruise ships, resorts, and travel agencies offer wonderful opportunities for hard workers who want to travel.

A job in the travel industry can be the start of an exciting career. The job can take you almost anywhere you want to go—Hong Kong, Alaska, New Zealand, even the jungles of the Amazon!

Seeing the world isn't the only reason to work in the travel industry. It's also a great way to meet lots of people. Many travel jobs require constant contact with tourists and travelers. Almost all are friendly and interested in having fun while seeing the world. It can be rewarding to help these people do just that.

This book contains seven interviews with people who have jobs in the travel industry. These people love what they do. And they have advice for people who are starting out.

While the jobs are all different, the people who work in them have similar personalities. Most travel companies are looking for people who are outgoing and friendly. That's the number one requirement. If you fit that description, then a travel career might be right for you.

No matter what type of travel job you get, it's important to have a desire to help other people. Being a quick thinker and an organized person is helpful, too. And since there's a lot of going on in the travel industry, the perfect person for a travel job is someone who

Many jobs in the travel industry offer a chance to see the world.

works well under pressure. And of course it's a plus if you love to travel.

There are countless opportunities for someone who is willing to work hard in a travel job. Travel is one of the biggest industries in the world, and it just keeps growing. Take advantage of it! There may be a job in the travel industry waiting for you.

TRAVEL AGENT

Nuts and Bolts of the Job

You're on vacation in Hawaii and everything is absolutely perfect. Your room is big and comfortable. The beaches are white and sandy. And the restaurants serve the best food you've ever tasted.

Who plans wonderful trips like these? It's the job of travel agents like Ingrid. She assists people with their travel plans. She books transportation tickets, reserves rental cars, finds the best tours and cruises, and reserves hotel rooms.

If Ingrid is making reservations for a business traveler, her job is either to find the most direct route somewhere or to create a trip package that will save the most money.

If she's working for people going on a vacation, her job is more involved. Not only does she look to save them money; she often advises them on where to go. "The **client** might give me the requirements of 'something adventurous in a warm climate,'" says Ingrid. "Then I have to sift through all the possible destinations and come up with the best travel suggestions."

The first thing Ingrid does when she gets into the office each day is to turn on the computer. The computer links her to the information she needs. Using the computer, Ingrid can pull up lists of airlines, hotels, rental cars, and even weather reports. If a business traveler calls in and wants to know what flights are available early Tuesday morning from Detroit to Los Angeles, she has the answers at her fingertips. She can tell the caller, for instance, that TWA has one at 6:30 A.M., Continental Airlines has

A travel agent's most important tools are a telephone and a computer.

one at 7:05 with only first class seats left, and United Airlines has one at 7:20. Without a computer, she'd have to make phone calls to the airlines and then call the client back.

Ingrid uses the phone a lot, too. Most of her clients call rather than drop by the office. And Ingrid also makes calls to find **wholesalers**. Wholesalers are people who buy all the seats on a flight and then sell them at a discount.

While much of Ingrid's day is spent finding the best deals, she also has to update travel plans. Airline schedules change all the time. Ingrid has to keep on top of those schedules to make sure that her clients get to the right plane at the right time.

Sometimes the ticket prices change, too. "If I issue a ticket at $280 and the price goes down the next week, I have to reissue that ticket and get the best price for my client," Ingrid explains.

Ingrid loves her job. She says that the best part about being a travel agent is hearing about people's trips. She works hard to create "dream vacations" and likes to hear that the client had a wonderful time. "It really makes me feel good to find out that all my hard work paid off," says Ingrid.

RELATED JOBS:
Real estate agent
Reservation agent

Sometimes being a travel agent is frustrating. A client might change his or her mind at any moment. "I understand if someone gets sick. There's not much they can do about it," says Ingrid, "but it's still frustrating. The part I hate most is when people just change their minds after I've done all the work."

Travel agents are often offered discount travel deals called **famtrips.** These are the trips that familiarize agents with vacation spots, tours, and hotels. Companies and airlines get together to organize famtrips. They hope the travel agents will be so impressed with a vacation spot that they will recommend it to clients. It increases business for the airlines and the resort area.

Ingrid says that famtrips are a great way to travel. She's been on famtrips to Saint Croix, Barbados, Jamaica, and on several cruises in the Bahamas.

Have You Got What It Takes?

Ingrid began working in the travel industry shortly after her first child was born. She wanted to spend some time away from home and thought the travel business might be something she could do part-time.

To learn the business, she took a night school course that taught her how to be a travel agent. The course wasn't necessary, but it was helpful.

Ingrid says that knowing about computers is also very important. "What I really should have done," she says, "is take a computer course. It's very tough to survive as a travel agent without a good knowledge of computers. When I was hired, I didn't know much about them at all. I learned very quickly, though, once I was on the job."

Travel agents should love to travel. There are lots of great travel deals that agents can take advantage of. "That's the benefit of being in this business," says Ingrid. "The pay isn't high otherwise."

Since most of the job involves dealing with people and making them happy, a travel agent should be able to communicate well. Being organized is important, too. You have to stay on top of the constantly changing flight schedules and prices.

"Most important," says Ingrid, "I listen well and take very careful notes. People usually know exactly what they want, and I have to give them that. I can't be sloppy, because I'm responsible if something goes wrong."

There are several things you can do to prepare for a career as a travel agent. Learn about the world. Study geography. Research good vacation spots. Then find where they are located on a map. And take a computer course.

You can also plan a trip for your family or a group at school. Make sure you think of all the details. Where do you want to go? How will you get there? Will you go by car? Ride bikes? Charter a bus? By planning small trips like these, you can develop the skills that a travel agent needs.

"I COME UP WITH THE BEST TRAVEL SUGGESTIONS."

TOUR GUIDE

Nuts and Bolts of the Job

The great pyramids of Egypt still loom large on the horizon, even though you're miles away from them. You've just spent the day at these ancient tombs. And the fun doesn't stop there. Tomorrow you'll be boating down the **Nile**! Each event seems more exciting than the one before. All you have to do is follow your guide.

Tour guides like Tom take groups of people all over the world. He works for Intrav, a tour company based in St. Louis, Missouri. This tour company focuses on tours for professionals and their families. "I've been everywhere," says Tom. "The **Far East**, Africa, the **Middle East**, Europe, South America. Everywhere."

Tom usually travels with tour groups to foreign countries. He first meets the group at the airport in New York. He gathers everyone together and handles the check-in. Once the group is on the plane, Tom doesn't have much to do. But he's always available if someone has a problem or a question. When the group lands at its destination, Tom helps people claim their luggage. Then he helps them through customs and arranges the hotel transportation.

From the time Tom meets the group, he is on duty 24 hours a day. But when the group is in a city, he transfers the touring responsibilities over to a person called a **ground operator**. The ground operator is hired by Intrav. He or she always knows the place the group is visiting very well. The ground operator takes the group to see local sights, museums, and restaurants. This gives Tom a little break, but he is still in charge if anyone has problems or questions.

"It's more important to know where to get the answers than to actually have the answers," Tom says. "Many times it's my first trip to a city. I don't know much more about it than the people in the group. But I can't let them know that. If I direct them to people who know a lot about the city, I look like an old pro."

A typical tour might keep the travelers in a city for four days. During that time, Tom makes sure people find the tours they want to take. He handles problems like lost passports. He refers sick travelers to local doctors. He also arranges dinners and cocktail parties for the group at night.

When the four days in the city are over, Tom arranges the trip to the next place. He checks the hotel reservations, gets **boarding passes** for the plane, and assigns seats.

"Assigning seats is harder than you'd think," says Tom. "Most airlines have rows of three, and most people on the tour are in groups of two. I have to make sure that the couples I split up are those who won't mind. And I have to make sure I put people next to other people they like," he explains.

RELATED JOBS:
Ground operator
Guide at a historical
site or tourist
attraction

After about 14 days of touring, Tom brings the group home. For two weeks he has been the link between the group and hotels, airlines, ground operators, tour guides, and restaurant people. He has coped with people getting sick, getting hurt, getting mugged, and even getting arrested. He's handled a lot!

Tom has had to deal with crazy situations that no one could have prepared him for. "We were on a trip to Africa once," he remembers. "Instead of staying in a hotel as we usually do, we were in a place called the Governor's Tented Camp. We were sleeping in tents, but it was very luxurious. We all had beds, and servants would bring us our breakfast and things like that.

"One morning, a servant was bringing me some tea and biscuits. Instead of setting everything up nicely outside the tent, as he usually did, he just stuck his head through the flap.

"'Stay in tent,' he said. 'Very bad elephant.'

"Of course, I didn't pay any attention. I stepped out to see what he was talking about." Tom laughs. "And there, about 15 feet away, was an enormous elephant with huge tusks. One shake of his huge head and I dove back into the tent!"

Being a tour guide has some great advantages. The salary is decent, and Tom gets tips from the people on the tour as well. When he's not on a tour, Tom still gets a regular paycheck. And he has a lot of time off. "I usually take about 12 two-week and 2 three-week trips a year," says Tom. "That leaves almost half the year free for me to do whatever I want and still get paid."

Tom says that the best part of being a tour guide is seeing the world. And he gets to stay at some of the best hotels and eat at the best restaurants. All of Tom's expenses are paid. If a group wants to go to the theater, Tom can send the people on their own, or he can go with them and the company will pay for his ticket.

Have You Got What It Takes?

A tour guide must always be in charge. Someone on a trip can have an emergency at any time. You have to be able to help—even if it's three o'clock in the morning! You have to take care of airline and hotel details. And you have to plan parties and events for the travelers. But if you like to take charge and solve problems, being a tour guide might be the job for you.

A TOUR GUIDE MUST ALWAYS BE IN CHARGE.

Tom grew up in St. Louis, where Intrav is based. He heard about the company from friends. He thought it sounded great, so he applied for a job. There was a lot of competition—about 300 applications for every opening—but Tom kept applying. His persistence paid off. Intrav finally gave him a job.

Tom believes that work experience is more important than education. And it doesn't really matter what type of work experience it is. It doesn't have to be in the travel industry. But you should be able to prove you're dependable and energetic. Tour companies are usually interested in people who have shown that they are reliable leaders.

Tour guides must also be friendly and able to perform under

A tour guide leads sightseers through a Tokyo shrine.

pressure. "For people who can demonstrate that they have these qualities, there's a good chance they'll be hired," Tom says. "A person's abilities are more important than any particular job experience or school."

Still, there are lots of things in school and at work that can get you on the tour guide track. Learning languages, geography, and history is very important. And high school is a good time to get experience in leadership positions. There are lots of possibilities. You can organize a sightseeing trip for people in your school. Coordinate schedules. Arrange for the bus. Collect the money. Pay the group's admission fee. If you like all that planning, then you'll love being a tour guide!

FLIGHT ATTENDANT

Nuts and Bolts of the Job

The plane jolts to the side. There's a lot of turbulence. Beverages spill and passengers panic. Why hadn't they listened to the safety speech before lift-off? Is there anyone who can tell them what to do? Joyce can!

Joyce is a flight attendant for United Airlines. She works on the **domestic flights**. These are the flights that fly within the United States. Her job is to help make sure that the passengers have a comfortable flight and arrive at their destination safely.

"Most people think we are there to ensure their comfort," Joyce says. "But that's only a very small part of it. We are there to ensure the safety of the passengers. That's our number one priority."

Joyce had to take a training course in order to become a flight attendant. More than half of that training session involved emergency medical procedures. Joyce learned **CPR**. She watched movies on how to deliver a baby. And she learned how to give oxygen to any passenger who might need it.

In addition, flight attendants need to know how to evacuate a plane in emergency situations. They have to be able to get everyone off the plane in 90 seconds, even if the plane is a giant 747 carrying 300 passengers.

When Joyce works a flight, she must get to the airport an hour and a half before that flight leaves. When she arrives, she gets briefed on the flight. The **brief** includes information like whether the flight is full and whether there are any passengers with special needs, such as small children or handicapped people. The flight attendants also hear about the conditions and delays on the runway.

After the brief, Joyce and the other flight attendants check the food, ice, and drinks. There has to be plenty of everything for all the passengers. If there isn't enough, the flight attendants have to get more. "It's awful to have to delay a flight because there isn't enough food or drinks," says Joyce.

Joyce usually flies on a 737, which is a fairly small passenger plane. There are three pilots and three flight attendants working on the plane. One flight attendant works in first class and the other two work in the main cabin.

After the plane is prepared for flight, Joyce and the other flight

RELATED JOBS:
Train conductor
Paramedic

15

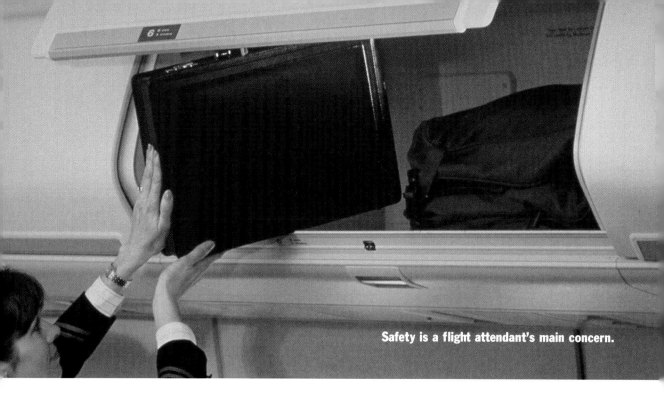

attendants check boarding passes and help passengers find their seats. They also make sure that all carry-on luggage is stored under the seats or in the overhead bins.

When everyone is on board and the plane is ready to leave the gate, the flight attendants give a safety demonstration and check to see that everyone's seat back and tray are in the upright and locked position. This is an important safety procedure.

While the plane is in the air, Joyce and the other flight attendants serve food and drinks. They also hand out pillows, blankets, magazines, headsets, and other items that passengers might want.

When the flight is over, the flight attendants help the passengers deplane. Then they make sure everything is cleaned up. They also check the overhead bins for anything that may have been left behind.

16 Once the plane is cleared, the flight attendants are finished with that flight. They often start the whole process over again with another flight. Flight attendants are allowed to work 16 hours in a row. Then they have to rest for at least 14 hours before flying again.

If a flight attendant has been flying for 16 hours and it's late at night, the airlines will pay for a hotel room. Many hotels have a separate floor just for airline people. Sometimes there are people from several different airlines on the floor.

Flight attendants place **bids** for their routes each month. That means they request the routes they want to fly. Sometimes they get the routes they want, and sometimes they don't. When Joyce lived in Chicago, she always bid for warm routes during the winter. "The best flight I ever had," Joyce remembers, "was the one going to Las Vegas. Everyone was always in a great mood. They were ready to relax, win some money, and have a great time."

Part of a flight attendant's job is making sure that passengers are comfortable.

According to Joyce, friendly passengers and co-workers make her job worthwhile. Of course, not all passengers are ideal, but Joyce has learned to cope with those who are less pleasant.

Sometimes flight attendants get to meet famous people. While working, Joyce has met Joe Namath, Tina Turner, and Bob Hope.

Another exciting part of being a flight attendant is the opportunity to travel. After working for six months, a flight attendant gets free passes to travel anywhere the airline goes. The families of the flight attendant get passes, too.

Have You Got What It Takes?

Being a flight attendant is more demanding than it looks. You're responsible for the safety of every single person on board. And you have to be polite and helpful to everyone.

When Joyce was about to finish school, she wasn't sure what she wanted to do. United Airlines was interviewing at her school, so she met with the company's representative. She thought it would be good interviewing practice. Once she passed that initial interview, she was sent to the main office, where she competed with 50 women for the spot. She must have been just what the airline was looking for, because she got the job!

Once Joyce was hired, she had to pass the training course. She learned all the safety and emergency techniques. And it wasn't easy! "It was hard enough getting everyone off the plane in 90 seconds. But then they pumped fake smoke in the plane and made us do the evacuation in the same amount of time. Some people just couldn't handle it."

Being able to hold up under pressure is one of the main requirements for a flight attendant. Flight attendants also have to be friendly, energetic, patient, and tactful. "You run into all types," says Joyce. "You have to be able to deal with a panicky older woman, a drunk businessman, and small children. And you have to be able to think on your feet."

When Joyce started out, there were strict requirements for flight attendants. They had to be a certain weight. They had to be female. They had to be pretty. And they had to be young. "I had to sign a contract that said that I would give up my job when I turned 32 or when I got married, whichever came first," Joyce remembers.

The unions have worked hard to change these requirements. Today, both men and women can be flight attendants. And flight attendants can't lose their job because someone might not think they're attractive enough. There is still a height requirement, but that's a matter of safety. Flight attendants have to be at least 5 feet 4 inches tall so they can reach the oxygen above the seats.

If you're interested in becoming a flight attendant, "Pay attention to your appearance. Not just your grooming, but also how you handle yourself. Make sure that you appear competent and friendly."

It's also a good idea to take basic first aid courses. Then you can volunteer for a local first aid squad or a local hospital. This will give you some safety and medical experience.

Or you can get a job in a restaurant. You'll learn firsthand what it's like to serve people. And you'll gain experience being cheerful and polite to everyone. If you feel you have a knack for these types of jobs, then you might want to consider becoming a flight attendant.

"WE ARE THERE TO ENSURE THE SAFETY OF THE PASSENGERS."

CONCIERGE

Nuts and Bolts of the Job

The New York Yankees are in town to play the Red Sox. They're staying at the Marriott Hotel. Who makes sure they are happy with their rooms? Who gives them breakfast? Who is there for conversation and advice? That lucky person is Joanna!

Joanna is a concierge at the Marriott Hotel in Boston. It's her job to offer people fun and exciting tips about the city. "I'm basically a cruise director on land," Joanna explains. "I tell people what to see in Boston and how to get there. I also recommend restaurants and get tickets for plays and sporting events."

There are two concierge positions at the Marriott: the lobby and the **VIP floor.** When Joanna works downstairs in the lobby, she assists all the hotel guests. When she works on the VIP floor, she helps guests who have paid extra for personal service. Joanna works both positions, trading off with the other concierges.

Joanna likes working in the lobby the most. "It's more active. Something is always happening, and there are loads of people around." Some of the hotel guests call down from their rooms with a question or a request. Others stop by the concierge desk. A guest might want Joanna to book a tour or get tickets for sporting events, concerts, or the theater. Or someone might ask for directions to another part of the city.

Baby-sitters are another common request. Joanna usually works with an agency to find sitters for people. If the request is last-

RELATED JOBS:
Cruise director

Chamber of commerce employee

20

Joanna enjoys working in the hotel lobby because it's always active.

minute, there might not be any sitters available. When this happens, the hotel likes the employees to step in. So sometimes Joanna's job includes taking care of guests' children.

When Joanna is working on the VIP floor, she acts as a personal concierge for important guests. "This floor is a fun place to work," says Joanna. "I've met some famous people. Jay Leno was here, and I once had a great conversation with Gregory Hines."

On the VIP floor, the concierge serves food and drinks. If you're working the morning shift, you serve breakfast. If you're working the afternoon shift, you serve cocktails and hors d'oeuvres. Joanna makes sure that both shifts run smoothly and that there is enough to eat and drink. She clears used dishes away from the eating area, so that the room doesn't look sloppy. During the cocktail hour, Joanna checks identification. She has to make sure that everyone who consumes alcohol is old enough to drink.

The breakfast and the hors d'oeuvres are free, but the guests must pay for their drinks. They sign a **chit** that lists their room number and what they drink. The drinks get charged to their hotel bill. "We trust them to be honest about the number of drinks, and usually they are," says Joanna.

On the VIP floor, Joanna fields questions that are similar to those she gets downstairs. The difference is that she tries to handle them herself instead of referring the guest to someone else. "If a guest has a problem, we try to solve it. In the lobby we refer everything. Upstairs, we try to handle it ourselves."

For instance, if a guest doesn't like his or her room, Joanna looks on the computer to see what else is available. She can also cut new plastic door keys if someone loses a key or wants an extra. If guests need extra pillows or blankets or would like their room made up at a special time, Joanna calls housekeeping for them. "We try to make things as easy as possible for the VIP guests."

Joanna enjoys being a concierge. Most people are friendly and interested in learning about Boston. And they appreciate everything that Joanna does. Joanna's advice about restaurants and tours makes a visitor's trip special. And that makes Joanna feel good. "I love hearing about what a great time people had here," says Joanna. "That's the best part of the job."

When a guest has a complaint, it's not as pleasant. Sometimes the guests come to Joanna with a problem she just can't solve. And even though Joanna can't do anything about it, the guests blame her. "It's very frustrating knowing there's nothing I can do."

But, on the whole, being a concierge is wonderful work. Joanna likes her job for another reason, too. "My family and I can travel to any Marriott anywhere in the world and stay there at a tremendous discount. It makes traveling a whole lot more affordable."

A concierge helps hotel guests check in and check out.

Have You Got What It Takes?

A good concierge is always learning on the job. Aside from knowing everything about the hotel, you have to keep up-to-date on new restaurants and attractions in the city. You have to know where to refer guests, whether they want a baby-sitter, extra towels, or a money machine. And on top of that, you have to be polite, cheerful, and helpful all day long.

Joanna began working part-time as a concierge while she was attending a two-year college to get her associate's degree in hotel management. She saw an ad in the newspaper and applied. She had all the traits the hotel was looking for, so she got the job. When she graduated, she started working full-time.

"The hotel degree is a plus for getting the job," says Joanna, "but it's not necessary. There are other employees here who don't have it. A high school diploma is a must, though."

It's important that a concierge be levelheaded. You have to be very tolerant, especially when dealing with difficult guests.

A concierge should also be outgoing and friendly. You have to be a problem solver. And you should be a good listener.

If you want to be a concierge, get to know the area you live in. Ask friends and relatives for advice on what restaurants are good. Go to as many as you can. Explore areas of your city that you've never been to. Take tours. You'll see the city, and you'll get a sense of which tours are the best. The more you know, the closer you'll be to becoming a concierge!

"I'M BASICALLY A CRUISE DIRECTOR ON LAND."

ASSISTANT CRUISE DIRECTOR

Nuts and Bolts of the Job

Pool volleyball in the morning. Harmonica lessons before lunch. And then there's the shuffleboard tournament in the afternoon. There are so many activities that you can barely catch your breath! And you still want to save time to watch the sunset from the ship's deck. Who has planned all of these great activities? Assistant cruise directors like Doug make every day on board loads of fun.

Doug works for the Royal Viking Cruise Lines. He and the cruise director coordinate all the social events on board the ship. Doug also leads some of the activities—anything from a game of bingo to a class on drawing cartoons to a nighttime cocktail party. Doug is also expected to mingle with the guests. "It's one job where you use all your interests and skills," says Doug.

Doug's typical day at sea doesn't start until around ten in the morning. That's good, because he's almost always been up late the night before. He usually begins his day in his office, getting some paperwork done and reminding himself about the events of the day.

Doug's first event is at 11:00 A.M. That's when he collects all the bets for the daily mileage pool. Guests pay $1 to guess how many miles the boat will sail that day. The winner collects the money.

After the pool, Doug will run an event like a golf putting tournament. There's a nine-hole putting course on board. Since Doug likes sports, this is an enjoyable event for him.

Then lunch is served. Doug is assigned to one table for the entire trip. He is the host of that table and eats there at lunch and dinner. He makes sure the guests are comfortable and keeps the conversation rolling.

The assistant cruise director organizes and runs activities for passengers.

After lunch Doug might take passengers on a tour of some part of the boat, like the **bridge**. Then he might run a bingo game. Bingo is very popular. Finally, he may hold a class on cartooning. Doug's two favorite activities are sports and drawing, so he tries to create events that suit his skills. After about three afternoon activities, it's time for the cocktail hour and dinner.

During the cocktail hour and dinner Doug is expected to mingle and dance with the guests. He also keeps an eye on the rest of the staff to make sure they are doing the same thing. "I remember one trip where a beautiful young woman was among the passengers," Doug says. "And she loved to socialize. It seemed like I spent all my time reminding the crew that they were ignoring the other guests."

After dinner there is more dancing and then there is entertainment, usually a couple of shows. Sometimes Doug participates in the show itself. But most of the time he is just the **emcee** for the event. He gets the audience warmed up and introduces the acts or performances. After the show there is a midnight buffet.

Doug works a very long day, and even after the socializing is over, he still has some work to do. He is responsible for changing the board that lists the events of the day. "I never get to bed before 2:00 A.M.," Doug says.

Despite the hours, Doug loves his job. Whenever the ship docks, he is allowed to do some sightseeing. He thinks that's one of the best parts of his job. He gets to travel all over the world!

Since the passengers are on the cruise to have fun, they are usually enthusiastic about his activities. "Each activity is rewarding in different ways, but the big reward comes from the passengers. They're the ones who make being here worthwhile."

Even though Doug loves socializing, it has its drawbacks. It's not easy being happy and cheerful all the time. Even if he is completely bored with bingo, for instance, Doug has to make the game seem like the most fun he's had in weeks. "It's hard to be 'on' all the time. Some days I feel like relaxing, being by myself, and reading a book. But I can't do that until the end of the cruise."

RELATED JOBS:
Camp director
Camp counselor

It's also tough not having a home for a large part of the year. Doug misses being around his family and doing little things like grocery shopping or watching television. "Most people love to travel on their vacation, but because of my job, I love to stay home."

A cruise director shows passengers around the ship.

Have You Got What It Takes?

An assistant cruise director has a lot to do. You plan and lead many of the activities on board. You socialize all day long. And you're often up until the wee hours of the morning.

Doug had an office job for a while, but sitting behind a desk drove him crazy. So when he heard about an opening for a sports director on a cruise ship, he applied. His interest in sports helped him land the job. He's been with the cruise line ever since.

After being sports director for three years, he moved up the ladder to social host. Then he was promoted to assistant cruise director.

An assistant cruise director needs to be outgoing, friendly, and organized. It's also important to be professional when you're on the job. "You can joke around with the passengers, but you have to take your job seriously," Doug says.

Socializing is a big part of being an assistant cruise director. So it's a good idea to keep up with current events. Many of the passengers love to talk about what is going on in the world.

Appearances matter a lot, too. Cruise lines usually look for people who are neat and presentable. So be sure to take care of yourself and pay attention to how you look. "You don't have to be drop-dead handsome or gorgeous," Doug says, "but a neat haircut and a body that's in shape will go a long way toward getting a job."

The other piece of advice that Doug has is to focus on skills. Figure out what you do best and then play that up in an interview. It could be that the cruise line is looking for just that skill.

Are you interested in becoming an assistant cruise director? Develop your leadership skills. Get involved with the student government at your school. Get active in a club. Plan a concert or dance at your school.

During the summer, get a job as a camp counselor. Many camp activities are similar to those that you would direct on a cruise. And while you're organizing a relay race or emceeing a talent show, remember that you're training for an exciting career!

"IT'S HARD TO BE 'ON' ALL THE TIME."

PASSENGER SERVICE REPRESENTATIVE

Nuts and Bolts of the Job

There's snow on the ground, and you can see a blizzard swirling outside the airport window. You stopped in Minneapolis to change planes, but now all the flights are grounded. Where will you stay? How do you get your luggage back? Who will help you in this strange city?

Passenger service representatives like Phil are there to help passengers in all kinds of situations. Phil makes things as easy as possible for the passengers before they take off and after they land. He checks baggage. He meets flights and tells people where their connecting gates are. He helps with customs. And he tries to locate lost luggage.

On a typical day, Phil goes to the airport and gets his flight assignments. He might have to deal with as many as five or six flights in a day.

When Phil meets a plane that has come in from overseas, he directs the passengers to customs. After the passengers get through customs, Phil helps those who need to make connecting flights to other cities. Phil has a list of flights and directs people to their proper gates. If there are any problems concerning luggage, Phil deals with that, too.

Once all the passengers on the flight are safely on their way, Phil deals with another flight. If there were a lot of problems with the first plane, Phil has to rush to be on time for the second one.

30

"I CAN'T TAKE ANYTHING PERSONALLY OR I'D BE MISERABLE."

Sometimes Phil has to deal with a departing flight. Some flights are **overbooked**, which means the airline has sold more tickets than the plane can accommodate. When that happens, Phil asks for volunteers to give up their seats in exchange for a later flight. He has to do whatever he can to get everyone on a flight and make everyone happy. "Every day it's a different problem," says Phil. "It's never boring."

Phil remembers one crazy flight on a Fourth of July holiday. There was a severe lightning storm in New York, and the planes had to be diverted to Montreal. When the storm finally let up and the planes could land in New York, all the passengers had missed their connections. Phil used all his skill and experience to hook everyone up with a flight.

One passenger was a pregnant Arabic woman who didn't speak any English. Phil needed to communicate with this woman because she was going to have to stay in a hotel and fly to her destination the next day.

A passenger service representative waits for people at an airport gate.

Phil didn't know any Arabic or anyone who spoke it. He thought fast and called the United Nations. Its office gave him the number of a translating service. But when Phil called the translating service, he was told he would be charged $200 for the job.

Phil thought the price was ridiculous. He couldn't authorize that expense. Then he had a great idea. There was an Arabic restaurant near his home. He called the place and asked if anyone there spoke Arabic. Luckily, he found a translator. Through the cook at the restaurant, Phil was able to help the woman get to her destination.

RELATED JOBS:
Flight attendant
Reservation agent

It's challenging for Phil to figure out how to solve problems like this one. That's one of his favorite parts of the job. "It's such a great feeling to know that you've solved someone's problem and they're happy about it," says Phil.

The other big benefit is travel. "The airlines have a lot to offer as far as travel is concerned," Phil says. "I've been all over the world, and it hasn't cost me much at all. My family flies free, too. All we have to pay is a service charge."

Have You Got What It Takes?

A passenger service representative solves different problems every day. You have to remain calm in high-pressure situations. If you are a levelheaded problem solver, you have the makings of a passenger service representative.

Phil was first hired by the airline as a temporary employee. He was a ticket agent. He liked working for the airline, so when a permanent job opened up, he took it. He gradually worked his way through the ranks and became a passenger service representative.

Airline jobs open up fairly often. "Even if the job that's available isn't the ideal one, take it," Phil recommends. Once you get your foot in the door, it's easier for you to get the job you really want.

"Being a passenger service representative isn't for everyone," Phil cautions. "To do what I do, you have to love solving problems. Someone who gets frustrated by problems would hate this job, because things rarely go as planned."

Aside from being a problem solver, a passenger service representative should be easy to deal with. It also helps if you're patient and have a sense of humor. "The airport brings out the best and the worst in people," Phil says. "And I can't take anything personally or I'd be miserable."

Passenger service representatives handle baggage check-in and seat assignment.

It's not necessary to have a college degree to do Phil's job. But a basic knowledge of computers and a good grasp of geography and languages are helpful. "If you know another language well," says Phil, "you can have your pick of jobs. It's great to be able to communicate with passengers on **international flights**."

If you're interested in becoming a passenger service representative, you need experience helping people. Get a job as a sales or customer service person in a retail store. Volunteer to work for a local charity organization. And if you speak a second language, practice as often as you can.

When it comes to personality, if you can think quickly and work well under pressure, you have the makings of a good passenger service representative.

CRUISE SHIP ENTERTAINER

Nuts and Bolts of the Job

You're cruising through the Bahamas. The day has been filled with sun, fun, and play. You've just feasted on a five-course meal. And now you're ready to relax and see some entertainment. The light dims. Four shadows appear on the stage. And then the show begins. Who is that performing before your eyes? It's Richard!

Richard is an entertainer on Carnival Cruise Lines. He sings and dances during the trip from Fort Lauderdale to the Bahamas.

There are three other entertainers that perform with Richard, making a foursome of two women and two men.

The group does three shows during the seven-day trip. One is a country music revue. One is a Broadway show. And one features pop and rock music from the 1950s. When he's not performing, Richard can enjoy the cruise. "I always describe the job as a paid vacation," says Richard. "Even though it really is a lot of hard work."

RELATED JOBS:
Theme park
entertainer
Cabaret performer

Because Richard's shows are at night, there is no specific time that he has to get up during the day. He can soak up the sun and join in the activities with the passengers. "Sometimes I'd rather be by myself, so I go to the library," Richard says. "So much of the job is socializing that it's nice to have morning time to relax and be alone."

In the afternoon Richard has rehearsal. During rehearsals the four entertainers work together to coordinate their moves and blend their voices. The longer they do a certain show, the easier it gets. But the entertainers always try to improve the show. So they often add new songs or dance moves.

The show itself is tiring, but Richard enjoys it so much that he doesn't think of it as work. "The only time that it's very difficult is during a storm." Richard laughs. "It's hard to keep up a dance routine if the ship is tilting!"

"IT'S HARD TO KEEP UP A DANCE ROUTINE IF THE SHIP IS TILTING!"

Musical revues are popular productions on cruise ships.

As an entertainer, Richard has other responsibilities besides performing. On every cruise, the captain hosts a cocktail party. The entertainers are expected to be there to socialize with the guests. "It's fun," says Richard. "Once you've performed, the passengers treat you like a star. They even ask for autographs."

Richard is always expected to be polite to the passengers. "The lack of privacy is the worst part of the job," says Richard. "Most of the people are great and I don't mind talking to them, but there are times when I just want to be by myself and I can't."

But Richard loves the chance to perform. "Singing and dancing are my favorite things to do," he says. "So it's nice to get paid to do them."

It's also nice that his work takes him to places like the Bahamas. On the days when the ship docks and the passengers go sightseeing, the crew and the entertainers always do a little touring. "We get to see things that tourists miss. I've really learned a lot about the culture and the history of the Bahamas."

Have You Got What It Takes?

Being an entertainer sounds like a lot of fun, and it is. But it's not a job that anyone can jump into. You need to be a talented singer and dancer. And once you're hired, you have to rehearse and make sure that your performance is the best it can be.

Richard had always wanted a chance to perform. Since he lives in New York City, it's easy for him to find out about job opportunities and auditions. He checked the want ads in a weekly newspaper called *Backstage* and found an ad for a cruise ship entertainer. He auditioned and got the job.

It helped that Richard knew how to sing and dance. But the

cruise ships are also looking for people who are outgoing and friendly. "Even if you're lying in the sun getting a tan, you're on the job," says Richard. "You have to talk to the passengers if they want to talk to you."

If you're looking for a job as an entertainer, Richard suggests that you read the newspapers that focus on acting. They have ads

Most cruise ships have musical entertainment for passengers in the evening.

for all kinds of performers. And there are jobs for all kinds of performers on a cruise ship. "We have magic acts, juggling acts, a **ventriloquist**, and a comedian," says Richard. "Find out what you do best and see if the cruise ship is hiring people with that skill."

It's also a good idea to try out for school plays or musicals. See how it feels to be on stage in front of an audience.

Start training early. The best thing you can do now if you want to be an entertainer is to take lessons in the kinds of performance that appeal to you. If you're a singer, take singing lessons. If you're a magician, study magic.

Work on any skill that you think a cruise ship might be interested in. Even if it's an act that the cruise ship has never seen, the cruise company might just love it and hire you.

FOUR THINGS TO REMEMBER NO MATTER WHAT TRAVEL JOB YOU WANT

1. Do your homework.

Now that you've decided what travel job might be best for you, you may wonder how you'll go about getting the job. First of all, do
your homework. Learn everything you can about the job. Libraries

have many books about the travel industry. Also, school counselors may have ideas on where to get more information.

The important thing is for you to be knowledgeable. If you know what you're talking about, employers will realize that you are serious about wanting the job. And every company likes employees who are well prepared.

2. Get yourself out there.

A job will never just fall into your lap. You have to make sure your face is seen by the right people. You have to apply for the jobs.

Type up a résumé. You should include your name, your phone number, and everything in your background that makes you seem like a good person to hire—where you went to school, your job experience, and any special activities you've participated in. Your interests and skills are also important, so be sure to include them if they relate to the travel industry. A sample résumé can be found at the end of this chapter.

Once you figure out your strengths, be sure to emphasize them. An outgoing and friendly personality is important in the travel industry. When you go for an interview, smile. Be upbeat and interested in what you're saying.

3. Find a mentor.

Another way to learn about the job is to find a mentor. A mentor is usually someone who can answer your questions and help to get you familiar with the travel industry.

Try to meet people who work in travel. Ask your parents and your friends' parents if they know people in the travel industry. Talk to those people about their job. Ask questions. And let them know you want to work in that field. They may be able to hook you up with an available job.

4. Work your way up.

Don't be disappointed if you don't get the exact job you want right away. Most jobs in the travel industry will help pave the way to a better job.

Even if your first job is a little boring, work hard and do your best. If you do your job well, people will notice. Soon they will give

Every year millions of tourists visit Versailles in France.

you more responsibility. Before you know it, you'll be working at a job you love!

The travel industry keeps growing. There are many opportunities for work. You have to start somewhere. And once you do, you'll be on your way to an exciting career in the travel industry.

Jake Peters
12 Maple Drive
Summit, NJ 07901
(908) 555-4321

Work Experience:

Waiter, T.G.I. Fridays

Served close to 100 tables during a shift. Juggled orders and kept customers happy when things went wrong. Solved problems in the fastest, friendliest way possible.

Lifeguard and Assistant Swim Coach, Summit Community Pool

As lifeguard, was responsible for the safety of hundreds of swimmers. Had to give orders and think fast in emergencies.

As assistant swim coach, was responsible for running practice when head coach was absent. Instructed swimmers in technique. Created activities to keep practice interesting.

Education:

Summit High School, Summit, NJ

Received high school diploma in 1990. Activities included varsity swim team (captain, senior year), Ski Club (treasurer), and American Field Service Club.

Have taken several courses relating to the travel industry, including geography, public speaking, introduction to hotel management, and introduction to computers.

Related Skills:

Fairly fluent in German
Familiar with computers

Personal:

Traveled to Germany, summer of 1989, with American Field Service program
Hosted Spanish student, summer 1988
Love to travel
Good under pressure

GLOSSARY

assistant cruise director A person who assists the cruise director, planning and running activities for passengers on a cruise ship.

Backstage A newspaper published in New York City that focuses on performance careers such as singing, dancing, and acting.

bid A flight attendant's request for a particular route.

boarding pass A card issued to airline passengers that allows them on the plane; it lists a passenger's flight number and seat.

bridge The control room of a ship.

brief An overview of the particulars of a flight, given orally.

cabaret performer A person who performs in a restaurant that provides entertainment for its customers. Cabaret performers often sing and dance.

camp counselor A person who supervises children at a summer camp. Camp counselors organize and run activities.

camp director A person who is in charge of a summer camp for children. A camp director hires the counselors, enrolls the campers, and makes sure that things run safely and smoothly.

chamber of commerce An association of professionals to promote commercial and industrial interests in a community.

chit A piece of paper on which a hotel guest records a purchase of food or drink that will be paid later with the hotel bill.

client A person interested in using a travel agent's services.

concierge A person who offers hotel guests advice and information about the city.

CPR (cardiopulmonary resuscitation) An emergency procedure that's designed to restore normal breathing after a heart attack or other life-threatening emergency.

cruise director A person who plans and runs activities for passengers on a cruise ship.

cruise ship entertainer A person who entertains passengers on board a cruise ship.

domestic flight Air travel within a single country.

emcee (also **MC**, for **master of ceremonies**) A person who is in charge of warming up an audience and introducing the acts or performers.

famtrip Discount trips sponsored by hotels and airlines to familiarize travel agents with new vacation possibilities.

Far East The countries of East Asia (China, Japan, and others) and the Malay islands. This term may also include India, Sri Lanka, Bangladesh, Burma, and Tibet.

flight attendant A person who is responsible for airline passengers' safety and comfort.

ground operator A person who is an expert in a certain city and can be hired to lead tour groups.

international flight Air travel from one country to another.

Middle East The countries of southwest Asia and North Africa, including Israel, Egypt, Saudi Arabia, Morocco, and other nations.

Nile A river in Africa that flows northward through Egypt.

overbook To issue too many tickets for the number of seats available, as on an airplane.

paramedic A person who works in a health field as support to a physician.

passenger service representative A person who assists passengers before and after takeoff.

real estate agent A person hired to sell houses and properties in exchange for a percentage of the money made from the sale.

reservation agent A person who assists customers with travel reservations, usually over the phone.

theme park entertainer A person who provides entertainment for visitors at a theme park such as Disney World.

46 **tour guide** A person who leads groups of people on trips.

train conductor A person who collects tickets and oversees the operation of doors on a passenger train.

travel agent A person who assists clients with their travel plans.

ventriloquist A person who uses his or her voice in such a way that it seems to come from somewhere else; the ventriloquist works with a puppet called a dummy.

VIP floor A floor in a hotel that is set aside for important guests.

wholesaler A person or company who buys blocks of seats at a discount and then passes on a small part of the savings to the passengers.

INDEX